BE A MAKER!

Maker Projects for Kids Who Love
ELECTRONICS

MEGAN KOPP

Crabtree Publishing Company
www.crabtreebooks.com

Crabtree Publishing Company

www.crabtreebooks.com

Author: Megan Kopp

Series Research and Development: Reagan Miller

Editors: Sarah Eason, Harriet McGregor, Tim Cooke, and Philip Gebhardt

Proofreaders: Claudia Martin, Wendy Scavuzzo, and Petrice Custance

Editorial director: Kathy Middleton

Design: Paul Myerscough

Cover design: Paul Myerscough

Photo research: Rachel Blount

Production coordinator and Prepress technician: Tammy McGarr

Print coordinator: Katherine Berti

Consultant: Jennifer Turliuk, Bachelor of Commerce, Singularity University Graduate Studies Program at NASA Ames, Former President of MakerKids

Production coordinated by Calcium Creative

Library and Archives Canada Cataloguing in Publication

Kopp, Megan, author
      Maker projects for kids who love electronics / Megan Kopp.

(Be a maker!)
Includes index.
Issued in print and electronic formats.
ISBN 978-0-7787-2575-6 (hardback).--
ISBN 978-0-7787-2581-7 (paperback).--
ISBN 978-1-4271-1763-2 (html)

      1. Electronics--Juvenile literature. 2. Electronic circuits--Juvenile literature. I. Title.

TK7820.K67 2016   j621.381   C2016-903327-9
                                                                  C2016-903328-7

Library of Congress Cataloging-in-Publication Data

Names: Kopp, Megan, author.
Title: Maker projects for kids who love electronics / Megan Kopp.
Description: St. Catharines, Ontario ; New York, New York : Crabtree Publishing Company, [2016] | Series: Be a maker! | Includes index.
Identifiers: LCCN 2016026029 (print) | LCCN 2016026373 (ebook) ISBN 9780778725756 (reinforced library binding) | ISBN 9780778725817 (pbk.) | ISBN 9781427117632 (Electronic HTML)
Subjects: LCSH: Electronics--Juvenile literature. | Electronic circuits--Juvenile literature. | Makerspaces--Juvenile literature.
Classification: LCC TK7820 .K67 2016 (print) | LCC TK7820 (ebook) | DDC 621.381--dc23
LC record available at https://lccn.loc.gov/2016026029

Crabtree Publishing Company

www.crabtreebooks.com   1-800-387-7650

Printed in Canada/072016/EF20160630

Published in Canada
Crabtree Publishing
616 Welland Ave.
St. Catharines, Ontario
L2M 5V6

Published in the United States
Crabtree Publishing
PMB 59051
350 Fifth Avenue, 59th Floor
New York, New York 10118

Published in the United Kingdom
Crabtree Publishing
Maritime House
Basin Road North, Hove
BN41 1WR

Published in Australia
Crabtree Publishing
3 Charles Street
Coburg North
VIC, 3058

CONTENTS

MAKE IT ELECTRONICS

Think it. See it. Build It. Share It. That is what the maker movement is all about. It is about dreaming. It is learning through hands-on, real-world experiences. It is working with others to find creative solutions to problems. It is about failing the first time and starting all over again until you get it right.

TINKER AWAY

Electronic devices are part of the maker movement. They are everywhere—from radios to TVs to laptops to game controllers. Each one of these **gadgets** owes its start to someone tinkering with a simple idea. Each one started with a maker.

MAKE A FAIRE!

Gather together all ages of tech-lovers, crafters, educators, tinkerers, engineers, students, and science clubs to share what they have learned and show what they have made, and you have a maker faire! The first gathering in California proved so popular that maker faires are now held around the world. Where else could you find new ideas and experiments in the fields of science, engineering, art, performance, and craft under one roof?

Electronics is part of the maker movement. Makers learn from others and by trying things out for themselves.

SKILL SETS

Makers need many different abilities and skills. Most can be learned. Math and science are key skills. So are communication, collaboration, and critical thinking. The most important skill that all makers need is inside each of us. It comes naturally. It is curiosity.

Curious people gather together in makerspaces where makers share knowledge, tools, and ideas. Makerspaces include libraries, schools, community centers, and the Internet. Another option is to try new ideas with friends and create your very own makerspace! Anywhere information and ideas are shared to help create a project is a makerspace. In fact, this book is like a mini-makerspace. Curious? Read on!

SAFETY

- Always work under the supervision of a responsible adult.
- Always wear safety glasses.
- Always follow instructions when using power tools.
- Never plug in electronics that have protective covers removed.

Always wear safety glasses to protect your eyes when you are working with electronics.

EVERYBODY'S ELECTRONICS

The maker movement is nothing new. People have been tinkering for years. And that is a good thing! Without all the background makers, the world of electronics would not be where it is today.

SEEING THE LIGHT

American scientist Thomas Edison was known for his investigations of a form of energy called **electricity**. He discovered that the carriers of electricity, called **electrons**, move in an airless, sealed container, or **vacuum**. This is called the Edison effect.

Using the Edison effect in 1897, British scientist John Fleming invented a vacuum tube. It was called a **diode** because it contained two **electrodes**. This was the invention that started electronics. Another scientist named Lee De Forest took it one step further and created the triode. How many electrodes do you think it had?

This photograph from around 1901 shows Thomas Edison in his laboratory. Edison used electricity in many inventions, including the lightbulb and the phonograph (record player).

SETTING THE STAGE

Stay with me! The invention of vacuum tubes was critical in the story of electronics. Vacuum tubes enabled the creation of radios, which began an electronic boom.

Development of other key electronic parts quickly followed from the late 1940s through the 1950s. Within the next 30 years, electronics would become an everyday part of our lives. New inventions made technology more powerful, easier to access, and inexpensive enough to afford.

MAKERS MAKING

Even in the early years of their development, electronics were not just found in scientists' labs. Curious tinkerers were taking apart radios and TVs to see what they were made from, and how they worked. Sometimes they improved them with minor adjustments. That is the thing about being a maker—it opens up new ways of seeing things. Anyone can learn about electronics.

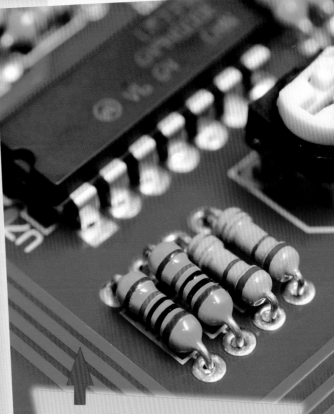

The different parts of an electronic **circuit** change, store, increase, or reduce the flow of an electric **current**.

Makers and Shakers

Sylvia Todd

Californian Sylvia Todd (born 2002) started making things when she was seven years old. She went to her first maker faire and was hooked. She now has a Web program where she shows people that making things is fun, easy, and rewarding. Sylvia is the creator of WaterColorBot. It is an electronic robot that paints! In 2013, at 11 years old, Sylvia was invited to the White House Science Fair.

ELECTRONIC VERSUS ELECTRICAL DEVICES

Electrical devices were in use for almost 100 years before electronic devices were invented. Italian scientist Alessandro Volta invented the **electrochemical battery** in 1799. Thomas Edison invented a number of electromechanical or electrical devices. They included the phonograph—a device for recording the voice and playing it back—in 1877 and a reliable light bulb in 1879.

THE LIGHTS ARE ON!

A good understanding of electricity and how it works is important for building a foundation for electronics. Electrical devices and electronic devices are different in the way they use electricity. Electrical devices take electrical energy and turn it into heat, light, or motion. Electronic devices control an electrical current in such a way that information can be added, such as sound and images.

The line between electrical and electronic devices can be blurry. Many electrical devices have electronic parts in them. Many electronic devices use simple electrical parts, such as batteries.

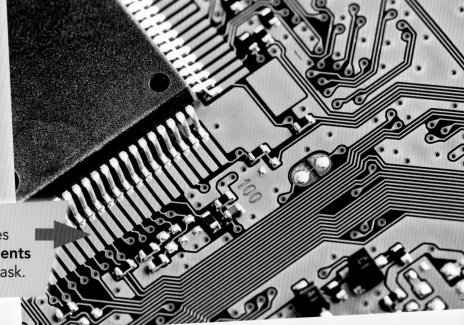

An electronic circuit uses many different **components** to complete a specific task.

SOUND CONTROL AND BEYOND

Electronic parts in your iPod turn electrical energy into sound energy. That flat-screen TV you are watching the Maker Show on is controlled by electronics. Electronics can also be used to make things happen when a **sensor** detects a lack of light, too much heat, or sudden movement. These types of electronics include automatic lights, a **thermostat** for your furnace, or a motion detector on the alarm system.

MAKING IT FUN!

Makers take electronics and build things such as simple lit-up nametags. MakerBloks use Lego-like, reactive building blocks and a tablet game to introduce young kids to the world of electronics. Orizuru is a paper crane that flies with the help of a mini-computer the size of an **SD card**. In Britain, more than 1 million tiny, wirelessly equipped computers—the Micro:bit—have been created for 11- and 12-year-old kids. It puts them in control of technology. The makers hope to shift the balance from kids using technology to kids creating with it!

Everyone uses computers, tablets, and **smartphones**—but makers like to think about creating technology, not just using it!

Be a Maker!

Thomas Edison worked with electricity during the birth of electronics. If he were alive today, what do you think he might be inventing? What do you think might be some common personality traits found in people who like experimenting and creating with electronics?

CHARGE AND CIRCUITS

Electronics need electricity to run. Just as water flows along a river and trains run on tracks, electricity does not travel aimlessly. If it flowed everywhere, we would all get shocked by it. Electricity and electronics need circuits, or closed pathways. Circuits provide a path for the current to follow. To be a circuit, the path must form a closed loop like a racetrack. Electrical circuits and electronic circuits are similar, but electronic circuits are usually low-**voltage**.

SIGNALS AND SUCH

There are two types of electricity. One is alternating current, or AC. The direction of electricity reverses constantly in AC. It alternates from one direction to the reverse, and back again. The other type of signal is direct current, or DC. Direct current flows in one direction.

SERIES VERSUS PARALLEL

There are two different ways you can wire things together in a circuit. One is called series and the other is parallel. When things are wired in series, they are wired one after another. Electricity passes through one component then through the next. In parallel, things are wired side by side. Electricity can pass through two things at the same time.

Series circuits and parallel circuits are the two simplest types of circuits.

Makers and Shakers

Quin Etnyre

Quin Etnyre (born 2000) runs a company that makes starter kits for kids who want to learn about electronics, especially Arduino (see "More Than Just Circuits," below). Quin started Qtechknow when he was 11 years old. His early creations included Fuzzbot, a robot that picks up floor dust with a cloth. Another invention was a fart sensor. More than a maker, Quin teaches teens and adults how to use Arduino for their projects.

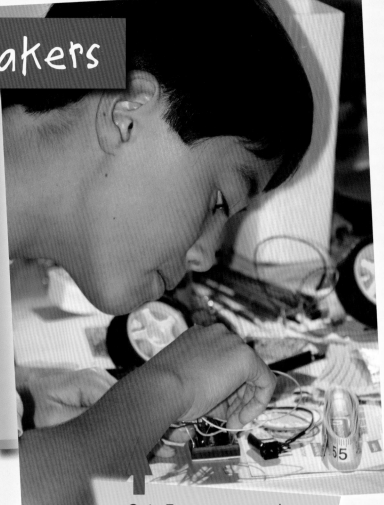

Quin Etnyre even teaches graduates of Massachusetts Institute of Technology about electronics.

MORE THAN JUST CIRCUITS

One popular circuit with makers is part of Arduino. Arduino is an inexpensive, user-friendly mix of circuit boards and computer software. It was created in 2005 as a teaching tool for design students. Makers quickly caught on to its usefulness. By 2011, more than 250,000 Arduinos had been sold around the world. Arduino can be used to make objects **interactive**. Makers can take a teapot and make it tweet or make a mechanical doggie door that opens by itself.

MAKE IT!
SQUISHY CIRCUITS

What is a squishy circuit? It is a fun way to build circuits and explore electronics by using play dough. The dough acts like a wire and **conducts** electricity from a battery to a light or whatever else is used. The dough can be shaped into figures that have eyes, noses, or fingertips that light up once the circuit is complete. You can work on your own or as a group—remember, great makers are inspired by **collaboration**.

YOU WILL NEED

- 6 V battery pack, with 4 AA batteries
- Snap connector
- 1/4 inch (5 mm) superbright LEDs
- 2 metal paper clips
- Play dough

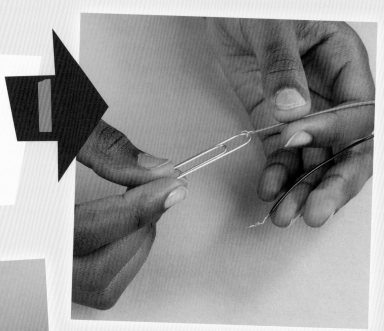

● Connect the battery snap connector wires to the paper clips. Twist the red wire around one end of a paper clip. Twist the black wire around one end of the second paper clip.

1

2

● Model your dough into two shapes.

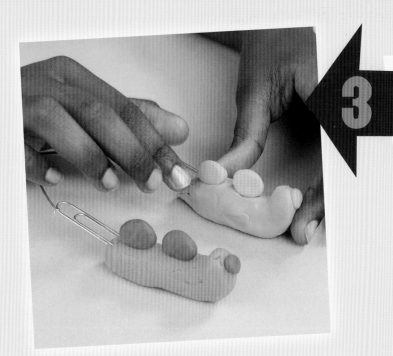

3
- Connect your paper clips to the dough by pushing them into each piece.
- Attach your battery pack to the snap connector.

4
- Insert your LED legs into the dough, one into each side. If your LED has one long lead and one short lead, connect the short lead to the shape that connects to the black wire. If your LED has a flat area on the plastic housing, connect the lead next to the flat side to the shape that connects to the black wire.

CONCLUSION
The LEDs light up because you have formed a circuit. You could shape the dough in any way you want, from animal shapes to machine-like parts. What other shapes might be fun to try?

Make It Even Better!
Study your creation closely. What worked really well? What could be improved or changed? How will you apply what you have learned about building a squishy circuit to the next circuit that you make? If you worked as part of a team, share your thoughts with your teammates.

TAKING ELECTRONICS APART

Boxed and shiny—that is how electronics look on the outside! But have you ever wondered what is going on inside that box and how those parts work? Tell your parents not to panic! We are not going rip apart the TV remote. We can learn about some of these parts from a safe distance.

RESISTING THE FLOW!

Resistors are devices that hold back the electrical current. They are the simplest part of any electronic circuit. Resistors come in many different shapes and sizes. Variable resistors—like the control on a light dimmer switch—change the amount of resistance.

CALLING ON CAPACITORS

A **capacitor** can be compared to a water storage tank. It stores electricity and releases it when the electricity is needed for use. Capacitors can be used for delaying the current flow for a period of time, like making a light blink. The most common capacitors look like tiny M&M candies with two wires sticking out of them. These capacitors work no matter how they are connected into the circuit. Another type of capacitor looks like a white licorice Good & Plenty candy with two wires coming out of the bottom or either end. This type of capacitor will not work if it is connected backward.

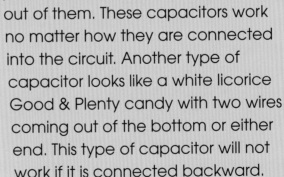

Capacitors come in different shapes and sizes (and colors!) depending on the job they have to do in the circuit.

TALKING TRANSISTORS

A **transistor** is a component that is controlled by an electrical signal. It is one of the most important parts in an electronic device. Transistors can switch tiny electric currents on and off, or they can be used to control current in a circuit. Transistors that work as switches are used in computer memory. Some transistors work as **amplifiers**, or sound boosters, in speakers.

Transistors like these have long "legs" so they can be connected into a circuit.

Be a Maker!

Visit a local thrift store and pick up a used radio or other old electronic device. Carefully remove the outer casing and look at the inner workings of the device. How easy is it for you to see a circuit? Look closely at the circuit. Can you see any resistors, capacitors, or transistors? If so, how many are there in the circuit? Does it look like a simple circuit?

DIODES

A diode lets electrons flow in only one direction. It works like a switch. When the current is flowing, the switch is on. If the current tries to flow the other way, the switch turns off. Diodes can be used to change AC power into DC power.

LIGHTING THE WAY

A light-emitting diode is called an LED. It is a special type of diode that lights up when electricity passes through it. Like all diodes, the LED has a positive end and a negative end. Electricity passes through in only one direction.

There are usually two ways you can figure out which direction electricity will pass through an LED. The first is by looking at the length of the wires sticking out of the bottom of the LED. The positive end has a longer wire. The shorter wire is negative. Sometimes there is a flat notch on the side of the LED. This points to the negative wire, but not all LEDs have this notch.

The earliest diodes used in electronic circuits were tubes like these. The electric current flowed in one direction inside a vacuum in the glass bulb.

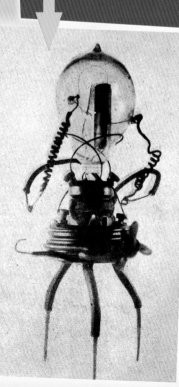

POWERED UP

LEDs can be used to show that a circuit has power. You find these electronic components everywhere, from the lights on your microwave to the clock in the car to your tablet charger. You can also use them for creations such as Bitcake. Bitcake is an electronic birthday cake with LED candles that you can blow on to make them flicker and go out.

LEDs are one of the simplest ways to show that your circuit is working.

Makers and Shakers

Joey Hudy

Joey Hudy (born 1999) was listed as one of the 10 smartest kids in the world. Since middle school, this Arizona boy's electronic inventions have been gathering attention. At age 11, he created a marshmallow cannon and shot sticky treats across a White House room with the president. He built a dog jacket called Dawg. It has lights that change depending on the activity level of your dog. At 16, Joey was working on "smart" glasses that work by reading human thoughts, rather than using a camera to sense eye movements. Joey's motto: "Don't be bored. Make something."

DRAWING CIRCUITS

Drawing the parts of a simple circuit helps us understand how a circuit works.

DISSECTING THE DIAGRAM

Diagrams of electronic circuits show the arrangement of components they contain. The power source is normally a battery for simple circuits. It is shown with two parallel lines, one longer than the other. The longer line has a plus sign for the positive terminal of the battery. The shorter line has a negative sign for the negative terminal. The voltage is sometimes shown, as well, for example, 6 V. The straight lines in the diagram represent the wire connecting each part of the circuit. The zigzag or wavy symbol represents a resistor. Variable resistors have the addition of an arrow pointing down to the resistor. Capacitors are drawn using two parallel lines. For some types of capacitors, a plus sign will be added near one line to show how to connect the capacitor in the circuit.

Diagrams of electronic circuits might look complicated—but, in fact, they only use a few standard symbols.

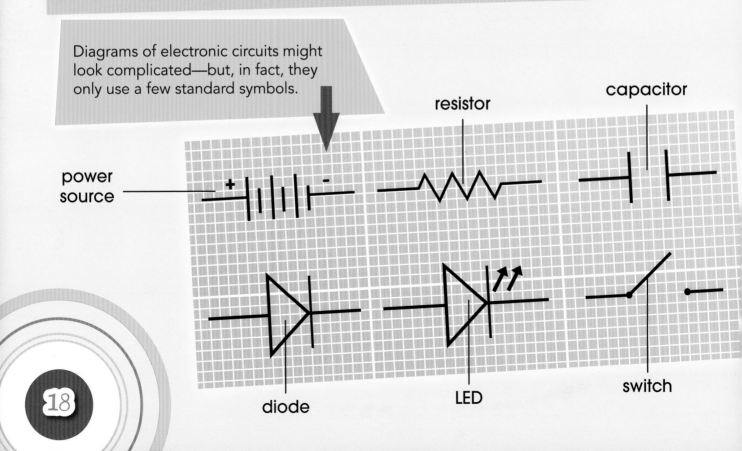

power source

resistor

capacitor

diode

LED

switch

Diodes are represented by a triangle joined with a straight line. Switches are represented by a circle and line. If the line comes off the circle horizontally, it means the switch is on. If the line comes off the circle at an angle, it means the switch is off. Dots where two wires (lines) touch show that those wires are connected to each other.

MAKE IT SIMPLE

Snap Circuits are kits that teach electronics with snap-together electronic parts. Each part has the electronic symbol and a color-coded label printed on its plastic case for easy identification. The pieces snap onto a plastic base called a **breadboard**. Completed projects look almost identical to an electronic diagram.

Draw diagrams to plan out your circuits before you actually start building them. (See page 31 for books and websites that show how to design circuits.)

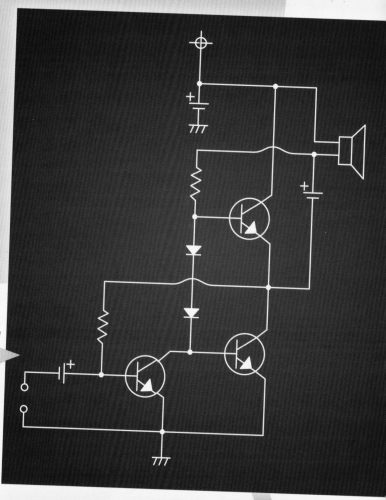

Be a Maker!

Makers learn and improve their skills and knowledge by sharing ideas with others. In what fun way could you share with your classmates the knowledge of how to read an electronic diagram? Do you know someone who might want to help you with a project? Work on it together! Share your thoughts about what worked and what did not work.

BREADBOARDS

Today's breadboard has little to do with the wooden kind used for cutting a loaf of bread. In the world of electronics, a breadboard is a platform that circuits are built on. When people first began tinkering with electronics, the parts were big and bulky. Wooden breadboards were the right size to attach components and start building circuits. Building the first version of a device came to be known as breadboarding.

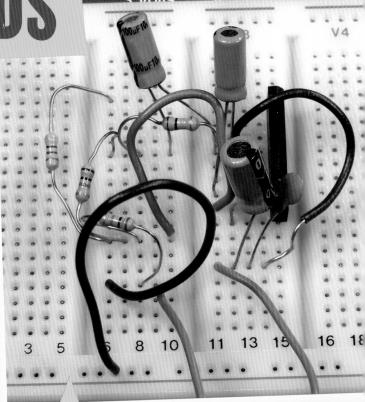

Each column in a breadboard has a number; each row has a letter. A combination of numbers and letters tells you exactly where to connect each part of the circuit.

SHRINKING SIZES

Since then, electronic parts have become a lot smaller. Building a circuit includes connecting parts with **solder**. It connects the pieces of the circuit together. There are electronic breadboards today that do not need soldering. These plastic boards are great because they let makers build, test, and analyze, then make changes, if necessary.

BREADBOARD BREAKDOWN

The back of a breadboard has rows of metal strips. These strips of metal allow pieces of the circuit to be connected electrically. On the top side of the board, you will see numbers and letters marked on the different rows and columns. The letters and numbers are guides to help build circuits.

Each row contains connected holes in groups of five. You build the circuit by simply plugging the wires into the holes. When you need to rearrange a circuit, you just pull the wire or part out of the hole and move it. Many books and guides have circuit diagrams for you to follow while building your circuit. Most breadboards also allow you to attach the circuit to a power source.

SAFETY FIRST!

Electronics use electricity. Electricity can be dangerous if it is not used correctly. Even small electronics can give you a shock if you are not careful. Be sure to keep your work area dry. Always wear safety glasses. Work areas should always include safety equipment such as a fire extinguisher, a first-aid kit, and a phone.

It does not really matter how untidy your circuit looks. As long as the parts are in the right order, it will still work!

Be a Maker!

Breadboards began as actual pieces of wood that tinkerers would use to hold their circuits. Plastic breadboards with numbered holes and easy "plug-and-play" function took over. What do you imagine breadboards will look like in the future? Will there still be a need for them? If not, what do you think might take over their role?

MAKE IT!
ELECTRONIC CIRCUITS

One of the best ways to learn about electronics is to build simple circuits. This circuit has just a battery, an LED, and a resistor. You can buy components online or in local electronic stores or hobby shops. Read all the steps and check the photos before you start building the circuit.

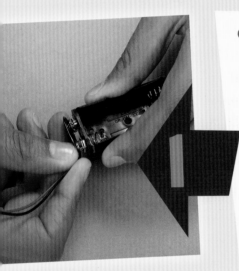

● Connect the battery snap connector. Insert the red lead in the top bus (power) strip of the breadboard. It may have a red line running beside the holes, and there may be a plus sign. Insert the black lead in the bottom bus strip. It may have a black or blue line running beside the holes, and there may be a minus sign. Any hole will do, but it is better to connect the battery at the end of the breadboard.

● Insert one wire of the resistor into any hole in the top bus strip. Electric current can flow through your resistor in either direction, so it does not matter which wire you insert. Then pick a row in the nearby terminal strip (the set of holes between the bus strip and the center of the board), and insert the other wire into a hole in that terminal strip.

● Connect the LED to the breadboard. Insert the LED into the same row as the resistor. Notice that one wire of the LED is shorter than the other. Insert the short wire into a hole in the bottom bus strip, then insert the longer wire into a hole in a nearby terminal strip. Check that the LED and the resistor are in the same row.

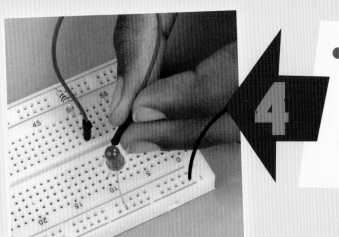

4 Use the short jumper wire to connect the terminal strips into which you inserted the LED and the resistor. The jumper wire will hop over the gap that runs down the middle of the breadboard.

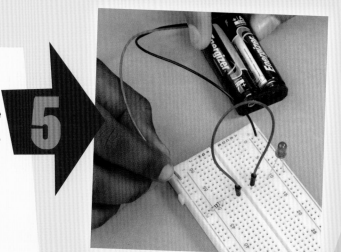

5
- Insert the battery in the battery holder. The LED will light up. If it does not, check your connections to make sure the circuit is assembled correctly. If it still does not light up, try reversing the leads of the LED (you may have inserted it backward). If that does not work, try a different battery.
- Do not connect the LED directly to the battery without a resistor. If you do, the LED will flash brightly—but then it will be dead forever!

CONCLUSION

Did you find it easy to insert wires into the breadboard? It is a simple skill to master—but one of the most important. It means you can start experimenting with building your own circuits.

Make It Even Better!

Easy peasy! Too easy? Flex your circuit knowledge and see if you can now build a parallel circuit, then a series circuit. What steps did you go through before you built your circuits? What had you learned from building the first simple circuit that helped you build other circuits? How will you carry forward this knowledge when working on future circuits?

INTEGRATED CIRCUITS

Makers take things and get creative. They share advice and build on one another's knowledge. That is how new things are developed. Hand-wired breadboards led to **printed circuit boards** (PCBs), which are platforms for building circuits and connecting components. Although these were an improvement, early computers still had to have all of their electronic parts put together by hand. No wonder early computers were so big, expensive, and unreliable. What do you think changed all that?

NEW CHIP ON THE BLOCK

Building simple circuits by hand is fun, but the power lies in **integrated circuits** (tiny circuits with thousands of parts). An integrated circuit, sometimes called a **silicon chip**, is an electronic circuit so small that it fits on a small silicon plate. Like a circuit, it is made up of transistors, resistors, and diodes. Special processes allow the circuits to be made in miniature. Even though they are super-small, integrated circuits are the building blocks of modern electronic devices such as tablets and cell phones.

TRIPLE THREAT

The 555 timer IC is one of the most successful integrated circuits of all time. It has 25 transistors, 2 diodes, and 15 resistors. A billion of these integrated circuits are made every year. You can create all kinds of timers and create sounds for alarms with this easy-to-use and extremely popular chip.

A single microchip like this packs many integrated circuits into a tiny space, so even complex electronic machines can be smaller.

THE FUTURE IS 3-D

Integrated circuits are not easy to make. They also take a lot of time and resources. They have to be made in a special factory by experts. In the future, **three-dimensional** (3-D) printing of these circuits will make it much easier for makers to create their own circuits. Design teams will be able to experiment more because they will be able to make tiny circuits themselves. If something does not work, they can change it and try again. Circuits will become part of the structure of an object. This will change how things look and operate.

An integrated circuit board looks a little like a tiny town, with roads and buildings.

Be a Maker!

If a friend asked you, could you explain how technological advances have changed the ability to build electronics? Where do you see these advances taking electronics in the future? What alternatives are there for makers who are interested in electronics but cannot access these kinds of modern materials?

FUTURE ELECTRONICS

Change is all about seeing something in a different way and pursuing it. Learning about electronics shows that change can happen when creative people get together and come up with new ideas. Researchers are currently looking at sending messages by **photons**, or packages of light, instead of by electrons. Light travels faster than electrical signals. Fast forward to the electronic future and the future is now!

SMART IS THE BUZZWORD

Creators are smart. They are making electronic watches that communicate with smartphones. Smart fridge magnets make phone calls, receive **digital** messages, and play music. There are smart trackers that know where your stuff is, and send you a message about it on your phone.

FUN AND GAMES

On the hobbyist side of electronics, makers are creating all kinds of things—such as electronic undershoes. These strap-on, electronic rollerskates act like the moving sidewalks you find in airports. They increase your walking rate up to 7 miles per hour (11 kph).

Stick me to your fridge

The Triby is a fun speaker that uses a magnet to stick to your fridge. It plays music or radio stations—and even reminds you to take out the trash!

triby

New makers are taking on projects such as the Hand Steadiness Tester. In this game, a player has to take a ring from one end of a course without touching it to the wire. LEDs light up each time the wire is touched, until the buzzer beeps and the player's turn is over. Smart stuff from makers just like you!

EVERYONE IS A MAKER

Engineers are makers. Programmers are makers. Hobbyists are makers. You do not have to have a degree in engineering or computer science to become a maker. You just have to want to do it, be willing to learn, and get creative!

Makers and Shakers

Limor Fried

Limor Fried (born 1979) is a maker's maker. It all started when she made her own MP3 player in a candy tin and put the how-to notes on her website. She was amazed at how many people contacted her asking for a kit. She thought maybe she should start a company. In 2014, Adafruit Industries was ranked number 11 out of all the manufacturing companies in the United States. It sells electronic kits, parts, and tools. The company also provides learning opportunities for makers. Limor, who goes by the online name "Ladyada," hosts weekly video shows about electronics. She chose the name in honor of Lady Ada Lovelace, the British woman seen as the world's first computer programmer.

Limor Fried passes on her skills to other makers in her video shows.

MAKE IT!
THREE-PENNY RADIO

Building radios is a popular maker activity. One of the simplest portable radio types to make was the three-penny radio. It actually used three pennies as part of the circuit. It is time to use what you have learned in this book. Your final activity is to see if you can put a modern spin on a three-penny radio.

YOU WILL NEED

- Ferrite rod 0.4 inches (10 mm) diameter, 6.4 inches (16 cm) long
- 65 turns of 28 AWG (0.3 mm) enameled copper wire
- MK484-1 AM radio integrated circuit
- Piezoelectric earphone
- Variable capacitor, 20–250 pF
- 100,000 ohm resistor (four colored bands: brown, black, yellow, and gold)
- 1,000 ohm resistor (four colored bands: brown, black, red, and gold)
- 0.01 microfarad capacitor (marked ".01M" or "103")
- Two 0.1 microfarad capacitors (marked ".1M" or "104")
- 1.5 V battery
- 1.5 V battery holder
- Solderless breadboard
- Electrical wire

- Before you start, place a small strip of double-sided tape on the ferrite rod. This will hold the wire in place. Wind the copper wire tightly around the rod.
- Place a small piece of electrical tape over one end of the wire to hold it in place. Keep the turns close together. You will need about 65 turns in all.
- Secure the last turn with a small piece of tape. Solder the ends of the wire onto two pieces of electrical wire. Place the ends in positions J9 and G16.

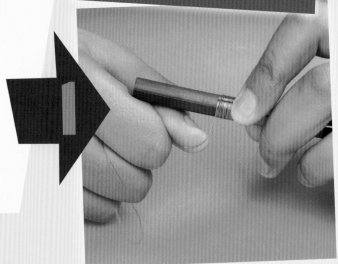

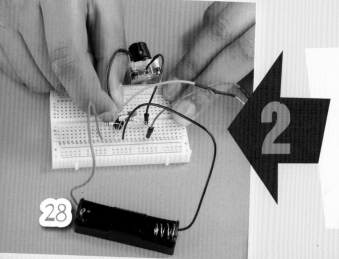

- Using two leads, solder the electrical wires onto the variable capacitor. Insert the wires into positions F9 and F16.
- Insert the MK484-1 IC into positions H15, H16, and H17. The flat side should face row G.
- Place the brown, black, yellow, and gold 100,000 ohm resistor into positions I9 and J17.

- Place the brown, black, red, and gold 1,000 ohm resistor into positions I17 and I20.
- Place the 0.01 microfarad capacitor into G9 and G15.
- Place a 0.1 microfarad capacitor into F15 and F17.
- Place a 0.1 microfarad capacitor into G17 and G22.
- Connect the negative black wire of the battery holder to position J15. Connect the positive red wire to position J20 on the breadboard.

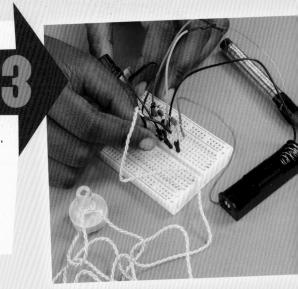

3

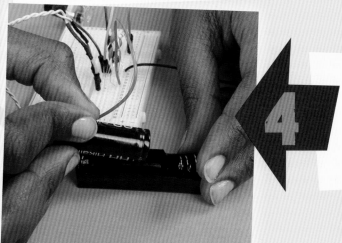

4

- Solder electrical wire on to the ends of the piezoelectric earphone and place these into positions F20 and F22.
- Insert a 1.5 V battery into the holder.

- Once the circuit has power, the electricity will begin to flow to the amp and the earphone. You should hear a sound, whether it is a faint radio signal or just static. This shows that all of your components are correctly connected.

5

Make It Even Better!

What elements of the project worked really well? Which parts of the project could be improved? If you worked as a team, do you feel you have created a piece that you all love? How would you change it or improve it?

CONCLUSION

If you live near an AM radio station, you might be able to hear it. If not, do not worry. Building a tunable radio is only a simple step further on this project.

GLOSSARY

amplifiers Electronic devices for increasing sound

breadboard A board on which an experimental circuit model is built

capacitor A device used to store an electric charge

circuit A path that forms a closed loop

collaboration Working with someone to make or create something

components Individual parts such as resistors, capacitors, and transistors that are used to build circuits

conducts Allows heat, electricity, or sound to pass through

current The movement of electricity through a wire

digital Information and images stored using binary numbers (1s and 0s) that can be used on a computer

diode An electronic device that allows current to flow in one direction only

electricity A form of energy caused by the motion of electrons

electrochemical battery A device capable of generating electrical energy from a chemical reactor

electrodes Parts in a vacuum tube or transistor that give off or collect electrons

electrons Tiny particles that move around the center of an atom

gadgets Small devices that do particular jobs

integrated circuits Small, thin wafers holding thousands of tiny resistors, capacitors, and transistors

interactive Working together or influencing each other

photons Light particles

printed circuit boards (PCBs) Thin boards that provide support for components

resistors Devices that limit the flow of electric current

SD card A small, secure digital card that provides large memory storage

sensor An instrument that can detect and measure changes

silicon chip A device that contains tiny electronic circuits built on a silicon plate

smartphones Cell phones that perform many of the functions of a computer

solder A soft metal that is melted to form permanent connections between the parts of a circuit

thermostat A device that controls the temperature of equipment or appliances

three-dimensional (3D) Having the dimensions of length, width, and height

transistor A device used to control the flow of electricity in electronics

vacuum A sealed space from which all air, or other gas, has been removed

voltage The force that pushes electrons and creates electric current

LEARNING MORE

BOOKS

Dahl, Øyvind Nydal. *Electronics for Kids: Play with Simple Circuits and Experiment with Electricity!* No Starch Press, 2016.

Monk, Simon. *Hacking Electronics: An illustrated DIY guide for makers and hobbyists.* McGraw-Hill Education TAB, 2013.

Platt, Charles. *Make Electronics,* 2nd edition (Learning by Discovery). Maker Media, Inc., 2015.

Scherz, Paul, and Simon Monk. *Practical Electronics for Inventors.* McGraw-Hill Education TAB, 2016.

Shamier, Cathleen. *Electronics for Dummies.* Wiley, 2015.

WEBSITES

DIY is a place for kids to discover new skills, including making electronics:
https://diy.org/skills/circuitbender/challenges/44/construct-a-pocket-amplifier

Instructables is a place where you can explore, make, and share your creations:
www.instructables.com/id/ChapStick-LED-Flashlight

SparkFun offers materials, classes, and online tutorials for electronics projects:
https://learn.sparkfun.com/tutorials/how-to-use-a-breadboard

Maker Faire is a family-friendly festival celebrating invention, creativity, resourcefulness, and the maker movement:
http://makerfaire.com

INDEX